MW01242644

THE
PYTHON BIBLE

VOLUME TWO

INTERMEDIATE AND ADVANCED

BY

FLORIAN DEDOV

Copyright © 2019

TABLE OF CONTENT

INTRODUCTION

I think I don't have to convince you that Python is one of the most important languages of our time and worth learning. If you are reading this book, I assume that you have already programmed in Python and know the basic concepts of this language. For this book, you will definitely need the foreknowledge from the first volume, since we will build on the skills taught there.

INTERMEDIATE CONCEPTS

So what can you expect from this second volume? Basically, we will dive deep into more advanced topics of Python but also of programming in general. We'll start with object-oriented programming, classes and objects. Then we will talk about multithreading, network programming and database access. Also, we are going to build an efficient port scanner along the way. After that, we will cover recursion, XML processing and other interesting topics like logging and regular expressions.

There is a lot to learn here and the concepts get more and more complex as we go on. So stay tuned and code along while reading. This will help you to understand the material better and to practice implementing it. I wish you a lot of fun and success with your journey and this book!

Just one little thing before we start. This book was written for you, so that you can get as much value as possible and learn to code effectively. If you find this book valuable or you think you have learned something new, please write a quick review on Amazon. It is completely free and takes about one minute. But it helps me produce more high quality books, which you can benefit from.

Thank you!

If you are interested in free educational content about programming and machine learning, check out: https://www.neuralnine.com/

1 – CLASSES AND OBJECTS

Python is an object-oriented language which means that the code can be divided into individual units, namely *objects*. Each of these objects is an instance of a so-called *class*. You can think of the class as some sort of blueprint. For example, the blueprint of a car could be the class and an object would be the actual physical car. So a class has specific attributes and functions but the values vary from object to object.

CREATING CLASSES

In Python, we use the keyword *class* in order to define a new class. Everything that is indented after the colon belongs to the class.

```python
class Car:

    def __init__(self, manufacturer, model, hp):
        self.manufacturer = manufacturer
        self.model = model
        self.hp = hp
```

After the *class* keyword, we put the class name. In this example, this is *Car*.

CONSTRUCTOR

What we notice first here, is a special function called _init_. This is the so-called *constructor.* Every time we create an instance or an object of our class, we use this constructor. As you can see, it accepts a couple of parameters. The first one is the parameter *self* and it is mandatory. Every function of the class needs to have at least this parameter.

The other parameters are just our custom attributes. In this case, we have chosen the manufacturer, the model and the horse power (hp).

When we write *self.attribute*, we refer to the actual attribute of the respective object. We then assign the value of the parameters to it.

ADDING FUNCTIONS

We can simply add functions to our class that perform certain actions. These functions can also access the attributes of the class.

```
class Car:

    def __init__(self, manufacturer, model, hp):
        self.manufacturer = manufacturer
        self.model = model
        self.hp = hp

    def print_info(self):
        print("Manufacturer: {}, Model: {}, HP; {}"
              .format(self.manufacturer,
                      self.model,
                      self.hp))
```

Here we have the function *print_info* that prints out information about the attributes of the respective object. Notice that we also need the parameter *self* here.

CLASS VARIABLES

In the following code, you can see that we can use one and the same variable across all the objects of the class, when it is defined without referring to *self*.

```
class Car:

    amount_cars = 0

    def __init__(self, manufacturer, model, hp):
        self.manufacturer = manufacturer
        self.model = model
        self.hp = hp
        Car.amount_cars += 1

    def print_car_amount(self):
        print("Amount: {}"
              .format(Car.amount_cars))
```

The variable *amount_cars* doesn't belong to the individual object since it's not addressed with *self*. It is a class variable and its value is the same for all objects or instances.

Whenever we create a new car object, it increases by one. Then, every object can access and print the amount of existing cars.

DESTRUCTORS

In Python, we can also specify a method that gets called when our object gets *destroyed* or *deleted* and is no longer needed. This function is called *destructor* and it is the opposite of the *constructor*.

```python
class Car:

    amount_cars = 0

    def __init__(self, manufacturer, model, hp):
        self.manufacturer = manufacturer
        self.model = model
        self.hp = hp
        Car.amount_cars += 1

    def __del__(self):
        print("Object gets deleted!")
        Car.amount_cars -=1
```

The destructor function is called __*del*__. In this example, we print an informational message and decrease the amount of existing cars by one, when an object gets deleted.

CREATING OBJECTS

Now that we have implemented our class, we can start to create some objects of it.

```
myCar1 = Car("Tesla", "Model X", 525)
```

First, we specify the name of our object, like we do with ordinary variables. In this case, our object's name is *myCar1*. We then create an object of the *Car* class by writing the class name as a function. This calls the constructor, so we can pass our parameters. We can then use the functions of our car object.

```
myCar1.print_info()
myCar1.print_car_amount()
```

The results look like this:

```
Manufacturer: Tesla, Model: Model X, HP; 525
Amount: 1
```

What you can also do is directly access the attributes of an object.

```
print(myCar1.manufacturer)
print(myCar1.model)
print(myCar1.hp)
```

Now let's create some more cars and see how the amount changes.

```
myCar1 = Car("Tesla", "Model X", 525)
myCar2 = Car("BMW", "X3", 200)
myCar3 = Car("VW", "Golf", 100)
myCar4 = Car("Porsche", "911", 520)

del myCar3

myCar1.print_car_amount()
```

Here we first create four different car objects. We then delete one of them and finally we print out the car amount. The result is the following:

```
Object gets deleted!
Amount: 3
```

Notice that all the objects get deleted automatically when our program ends. But we can manually delete them before that happens by using the *del* keyword.

HIDDEN ATTRIBUTES

If we want to create *hidden* attributes that can only be accessed within the class, we can do this with *underlines*.

```
class MyClass:

    def __init__(self):
        self.__hidden = "Hello"
        print(self.__hidden) # Works

m1 = MyClass()
print(m1.__hidden) # Doesn't Work
```

By putting two underlines before the attribute name, we make it invisible from outside the class. The first print function works because it is inside of the class. But when we try to access this attribute from the object, we can't.

INHERITANCE

One very important and powerful concept of object-oriented programming is *inheritance*. It allows us to use existing classes and to extend them with new attributes and functions.

For example, we could have the *parent class* which represents a *Person* and then we could have many *child classes* like *Dancer, Policeman, Artist* etc. All of these would be considered a person and they would have the same basic attributes. But they are special kinds of persons with more attributes and functions.

```python
class Person:

    def __init__(self, name, age):
        self.name = name
        self.age = age

    def get_older(self, years):
        self.age += years

class Programmer(Person):

    def __init__(self, name, age, language):
        super(Programmer, self).__init__(name, age)
        self.language = language

    def print_language(self):
        print("Favorite Programming Language: {}"
            .format(self.language))
```

You can see that we created two classes here. The first one is the *Person* class, which has the attributes *name* and *age*. Additionally, it has a function *get_older* that increases the age.

The second class is the *Programmer* class and it inherits from the *Person* class. This is stated in the parentheses after the class name. In the constructor we have one additional attribute *language*. First we need to pass our class to the *super* function. This function allows us to call the constructor of the parent class *Person*. There we pass our first two parameters. We also have an additional function *print_language*.

```
p1 = Programmer("Mike", 30, "Python")

print(p1.age)
print(p1.name)
print(p1.language)

p1.get_older(5)

print(p1.age)
```

Our *Programmer* object can now access all the attributes and functions of its parent class, additionally to its new values. These are the results of the statements:

```
30
Mike
Python
35
```

Overwriting Methods

When one class inherits from another class, it can overwrite its methods. This is automatically done by defining a method with the same name and the same amount of parameters.

```python
class Animal:

    def __init__(self, name):
        self.name = name

    def make_sound(self):
        print("Some sound!")

class Dog(Animal):

    def __init__(self, name):
        super(Dog, self).__init__(name)

    def make_sound(self):
        print("Bark!")
```

Here the function *make_sound* was overwritten in the child class *Dog*. It now has a different functionality than the function of the parent class *Animal*.

Operator Overloading

When we create a class with various attributes, it is not clear what should happen when we perform certain operations on them. For example, what should happen when we add two humans or when we multiply them? Since there is no default solution for this question, we can *overload* and define the operators ourselves. That allows us to choose what happens when we apply the operators on our objects.

```python
class Vector():

    def __init__(self, x, y):
        self.x = x
        self.y = y

    def __str__(self):
        return "X: %d, Y: %d" % (self.x,
                                 self.y)

    def __add__(self, other):
        return Vector(self.x + other.x,
                      self.y + other.y)

    def __sub__(self, other):
        return Vector(self.x - other.x,
                      self.y - other.y)
```

Here you see a class that represents the function of a *Vector*. When you add a vector to another, you need to add the individual values. This is the same for subtracting. If you don't know what vectors are mathematically, forget about them. This is just one example.

We use the functions __*add*__ and __*sub*__ to define what happens when we apply the + and the − operator. The __*str*__ function determines what happens when we print the object.

```
v1 = Vector(3, 5)
v2 = Vector(6, 2)
v3 = v1 + v2
v4 = v1 - v2

print(v1)
print(v2)
print(v3)
print(v4)
```

The results are the following:

```
X: 3, Y: 5
X: 6, Y: 2
X: 9, Y: 7
X: -3, Y: 3
```

2 – MULTITHREADING

Threads are lightweight processes that perform certain actions in a program and they are part of a process themselves. These threads can work in parallel with each other in the same way as two individual applications can.

Since threads in the same process share the memory space for the variables and the data, they can exchange information and communicate efficiently. Also, threads need fewer resources than processes. That's why they're often called lightweight processes.

HOW A THREAD WORKS

A thread has a beginning or a start, a working sequence and an end. But it can also be stopped or put on hold at any time. The latter is also called *sleep*.

There are two types of threads: *Kernel Threads* and *User Threads*. Kernel threads are part of the operating system, whereas user threads are managed by the programmer. That's why we will focus on user threads in this book.

In Python, a thread is a class that we can create instances of. Each of these instances then represents an individual thread which we can start, pause or stop. They are all independent from each other and they can perform different operations at the same time.

For example, in a video game, one thread could be rendering all the graphics, while another thread processes the keyboard and mouse inputs. It would be unthinkable to serially perform these tasks one after the other.

STARTING THREADS

In order to work with threads in Python, we will need to import the respective library *threading*.

```python
import threading
```

Then, we need to define our target function. This will be the function that contains the code that our thread shall be executing. Let's just keep it simple for the beginning and write a *hello world* function.

```python
import threading

def hello():
    print("Hello World!")

t1 = threading.Thread(target=hello)
t1.start()
```

After we have defined the function, we create our first thread. For this, we use the class *Thread* of the imported *threading* module. As a parameter, we specify the *target* to be the *hello* function. Notice that we don't put parentheses after our function name here, since we are not calling it but just referring to it. By using the *start* method we put our thread to work and it executes our function.

START VS RUN

In this example, we used the function *start* to put our thread to work. Another alternative would be the function *run*. The difference between these two functions gets important, when we are dealing with more than just one thread.

When we use the *run* function to execute our threads, they run serially one after the other. They wait for each other to finish. The *start* function puts all of them to work simultaneously.

The following example demonstrates this difference quite well.

```python
import threading

def function1():
    for x in range(1000):
        print("ONE")

def function2():
    for x in range(1000):
        print("TWO")

t1 = threading.Thread(target=function1)
t2 = threading.Thread(target=function2)
t1.start()
t2.start()
```

When you run this script, you will notice that the output alternates between *ONEs* and *TWOs*. Now if you use the *run* function instead of the *start* function, you will see 1000 times *ONE* followed by 1000 times *TWO*. This shows you that the threads are run serially and not in parallel.

One more thing that you should know is that the application itself is also the main thread, which continues to run in the background. So while your threads are running, the code of the script will be executed unless you wait for the threads to finish.

WAITING FOR THREADS

If we want to wait for our threads to finish before we move on with the code, we can use the *join* function.

```python
import threading

def function():
    for x in range(500000):
        print("HELLO WORLD!")

t1 = threading.Thread(target=function)
t1.start()

print("THIS IS THE END!")
```

If you execute this code, you will start printing the text *"HELLO WORLD!"* 500,000 times. But what you will notice is that the last print statement gets executed immediately after our thread starts and not after it ends.

```python
t1 = threading.Thread(target=function)
t1.start()

t1.join()

print("THIS IS THE END!")
```

By using the *join* function here, we wait for the thread to finish before we move on with the last print statement. If we want to set a maximum time that we want to wait, we just pass the number of seconds as a parameter.

```
t1 = threading.Thread(target=function)
t1.start()

t1.join(5)

print("THIS IS THE END!")
```

In this case, we will wait for the thread to finish but only a maximum of five seconds. After this time has passed we will proceed with the code.

Notice that we are only waiting for this particular thread. If we would have other threads running at the same time, we would have to call the *join* function on each of them in order to wait for all of them.

THREAD CLASSES

Another way to build our threads is to create a class that inherits the *Thread* class. We can then modify the *run* function and implement our functionality. The *start* function is also using the code from the *run* function so we don't have to worry about that.

```python
import threading

class MyThread(threading.Thread):

    def __init__(self, message):
        threading.Thread.__init__(self)
        self.message = message

    def run(self):
        for x in range(100):
            print(self.message)

mt1 = MyThread("This is my thread message!")
mt1.start()
```

It is basically the same but it offers more modularity and structure, if you want to use attributes and additional functions.

SYNCHRONIZING THREADS

Sometimes you are going to have multiple threads running that all try to access the same resource. This may lead to inconsistencies and problems. In order to prevent such things there is a concept called *locking*. Basically, one thread is locking all of the other threads and they can only continue to work when the lock is removed.

I came up with the following quite trivial example. It seems a bit abstract but you can still get the concept here.

```python
import threading
import time

x = 8192

def halve():
    global x
    while(x > 1):
        x /= 2
        print(x)
        time.sleep(1)
    print("END!")

def double():
    global x
    while(x < 16384):
        x *= 2
        print(x)
        time.sleep(1)
    print("END!")

t1 = threading.Thread(target=halve)
t2 = threading.Thread(target=double)

t1.start()
t2.start()
```

Here we have two functions and the variable x that starts at the value *8192*. The first function halves the number as long as it is greater than one, whereas the second function doubles the number as long as it is less than *16384*.

Also, I've imported the module *time* in order to use the function *sleep*. This function puts the thread to sleep for a couple of seconds (in this case one second). So it pauses. We just do that, so that we can better track what's happening.

When we now start two threads with these target functions, we will see that the script won't come to an end. The *halve* function will constantly decrease the number and the *double* function will constantly increase it.

With locking we can now let one function finish before the next function starts. Of course, in this example this is not very useful but we can do the same thing in much more complex situations.

```python
import threading
import time

x = 8192

lock = threading.Lock()

def halve():
    global x, lock
    lock.acquire()
    while(x > 1):
        x /= 2
        print(x)
        time.sleep(1)
    print("END!")
    lock.release()

def double():
    global x, lock
    lock.acquire()
    while(x < 16384):
        x *= 2
        print(x)
        time.sleep(1)
    print("END!")
    lock.release()

t1 = threading.Thread(target=halve)
t2 = threading.Thread(target=double)

t1.start()
t2.start()
```

So here we added a couple of elements. First of all we defined a *Lock* object. It is part of the *threading* module and we need this object in order to manage the locking.

Now, when we want to try to lock the resource, we use the function *acquire*. If the lock was already locked by someone else, we wait until it is released again before we continue with the code. However, if the lock is free, we lock it ourselves and release it at the end using the *release* function.

Here, we start both functions with a locking attempt. The first function that gets executed will lock the other function and finish its loop. After that it will release the lock and the other function can do the same.

So the number will be halved until it reaches the number one and then it will be doubled until it reaches the number *16384*.

SEMAPHORES

Sometimes we don't want to completely lock a resource but just limit it to a certain amount of threads or accesses. In this case, we can use so-called *semaphores*.

To demonstrate this concept, we will look at another very abstract example.

```python
import threading
import time

semaphore = threading.BoundedSemaphore(value=5)

def access(thread_number):
    print("{}: Trying access..."
            .format(thread_number))
    semaphore.acquire()
    print("{}: Access granted!"
            .format(thread_number))
    print("{}: Waiting 5 seconds..."
            .format(thread_number))
    time.sleep(5)
    semaphore.release()
    print("{}: Releasing!"
            .format(thread_number))

for thread_number in range(10):
    t = threading.Thread(target=access,
                            args=(thread_number,))
    t.start()
```

We first use the *BoundedSemaphore* class to create our *semaphore* object. The parameter *value* determines how many parallel accesses we allow. In this case, we choose five.

With our *access* function, we try to access the semaphore. Here, this is also done with the *acquire* function. If there are less than five threads utilizing the semaphore, we can acquire it and continue with the code. But when it's full, we need to wait until some other thread frees up one space.

When we run this code, you will see that the first five threads will immediately run the code, whereas the remaining five threads will need to wait five seconds until the first threads *release* the semaphore.

This process makes a lot of sense when we have limited resources or limited computational power in a system and we want to limit the access to it.

EVENTS

With *events* we can manage our threads even better. We can pause a thread and wait for a certain *event* to happen, in order to continue it.

```python
import threading

event = threading.Event()

def function():
    print("Waiting for event...")
    event.wait()
    print("Continuing!")

thread = threading.Thread(target=function)
thread.start()

x = input("Trigger event?")
if(x == "yes"):
    event.set()
```

To define an *event* we use the *Event* class of the *threading* module. Now we define our *function* which waits for our event. This is done with the *wait* function. So we start the thread and it waits.

Then we ask the user, if he wants to trigger the event. If the answer is yes, we trigger it by using the *set* function. Once the event is triggered, our function no longer waits and continues with the code.

DAEMON THREADS

So-called *daemon threads* are a special kind of thread that runs in the background. This means that the program can be terminated even if this thread is still running. Daemon threads are typically used for background tasks like synchronizing, loading or cleaning up files that are not needed anymore. We define a thread as a *daemon* by setting the respective parameter in the constructor for *Thread* to *True*.

```python
import threading
import time

path = "text.txt"
text = ""

def readFile():
    global path, text
    while True:
        with open(path) as file:
            text = file.read()
        time.sleep(3)

def printloop():
    global text
    for x in range(30):
        print(text)
        time.sleep(1)
```

```
t1 = threading.Thread(target=readFile,
daemon=True)
t2 = threading.Thread(target=printloop)

t1.start()
t2.start()
```

So, here we have two functions. The first one
constantly reads in the text from a file and saves it
into the *text* variable. This is done in an interval of
three seconds. The second one prints out the content
of *text* every second but only 30 times.

As you can see, we start the *readFile* function in a
daemon thread and the *printloop* function in an
ordinary thread. So when we run this script and
change the content of the *text.txt* file while it is
running, we will see that it prints the actual content all
the time. Of course, we first need to create that file
manually.

After it printed the content 30 times however, the
whole script will stop, even though the daemon
thread is still reading in the files. Since the ordinary
threads are all finished, the program ends and the
daemon   thread   just   gets   terminated.

---

3 – QUEUES

In Python, *queues* are structures that take in data in a certain order to then output it in a certain order. The default queue type is the so-called *FIFO queue*. This stands for *first in first out* and the name describes exactly what it does. The elements that enter the queue first are also the elements that will leave the queue first.

```python
import queue

q = queue.Queue()

for x in range(5):
    q.put(x)

for x in range(5):
    print(q.get(x))
```

In order to work with queues in Python, we need to import the module *queue*. We can then create an instance of the class *Queue* by using the constructor.

As you can see, we are using two functions here – *put* and *get*. The *put* function adds an element to the queue that can then be extracted by the *get* function.

Here, we put in the numbers one to five into our queue. Then, we just get the elements and print them. The order stays the same, since the default queue is *FIFO*.

Queuing Resources

Let's say we have a list of numbers that need to be processed. We decide to use multiple threads, in order to speed up the process. But there might be a problem. The threads don't know which number has already been processed and they might do the same work twice, which would be unnecessary. Also, solving the problem with a counter variable won't always work, because too many threads access the same variable and numbers might get skipped.

In this case we can just use queues to solve our problems. We fill up our queue with the numbers and every thread just uses the *get* function, to get the next number and process it.

Let's say we have the following *worker* function:

```python
import threading
import queue
import math

q = queue.Queue()
threads = []

def worker():
    while True:
        item = q.get()
        if item is None:
            break
        print(math.factorial(item))
        q.task_done()
```

We start out with an empty queue and an empty list for threads. Our function has an endless loop that gets numbers from the list and calculates the factorial of them. For this *factorial* function, we need to import the module *math*. But you can ignore this part, since it is only used because the computation requires a lot of resources and takes time. At the end, we use the function *task_done* of the queue, in order to signal that the element was processed.

```
for x in range(5):
    t = threading.Thread(target=worker)
    t.start()
    threads.append(t)

zahlen = [134000, 14, 5, 300, 98, 88, 11, 23]

for item in zahlen:
    q.put(item)

q.join()

for i in range(5):
    q.put(None)
```

We then use a for loop to create and start five threads that we also add to our list. After that, we create a list of numbers, which we then all put into the queue.

The method *join* of the *queue* waits for all elements to be extracted and processed. Basically, it waits for all the *task_done* functions. After that, we put *None* elements into the queue, so that our loops break.

Notice that our threads can't process the same element twice or even skip one because they can only get them by using the *get* function.

If we would use a counter for this task, two threads might increase it at the same time and then skip an element. Or they could just access the same element simultaneously. Queues are irreplaceable for tasks like this. We will see a quite powerful application of queues in the chapter about *networking*.

LIFO QUEUES

An alternative to the *FIFO queues* would be the *LIFO queues*. That stands for *last in first out*. You can imagine this queue like some sort of stack. The element you put last on top of the stack is the first that you can get from it.

```python
import queue

q = queue.LifoQueue()

numbers = [1, 2, 3, 4, 5]

for x in numbers:
    q.put(x)

while not q.empty():
    print(q.get())
```

By using the *LifoQueue* class from the *queue* module, we can create an instance of this type. When we now put in the numbers one to five in ascending order, we will get them back in descending order.

The result would be:

```
5   4   3   2   1
```

PRIORITIZING QUEUES

What we can also do in Python, is creating *prioritized queues*. In these, every element gets assigned a level of priority that determines when they will leave the queue.

```python
import queue

q = queue.PriorityQueue()

q.put((8, "Some string"))
q.put((1, 2023))
q.put((90, True))
q.put((2, 10.23))

while not q.empty():
    print(q.get())
```

Here, we create a new instance of the class *PriorityQueue*. When we put a new element into this queue, we need to pass a *tuple* as a parameter. The first element of the tuple is the level of importance (the lower the number, the higher the priority) and the second element is the actual object or value that we want to put into the queue.

When we execute the print statement of the loop, we get the following results:

```
(1, 2023)
(2, 10.23)
(8, 'Some string')
(90, True)
```

As you can see, the elements got sorted by their priority number. If you only want to access the actual value, you need to address the index one because it is the second value of the tuple.

```
while not q.empty():
    print(q.get()[1])
```

4 – Network Programming

Now we get into one of the most interesting intermediate topics – *network programming*. It is about communicating with other applications and devices via some network. That can be the internet or just the local area network.

Sockets

What Are Sockets?

Whenever we talk about networking in programming, we also have to talk about *sockets*. They are the endpoints of the communication channels or basically, the endpoints that talk to each other. The communication may happen in the same process or even across different continents over the internet.

What's important is that in Python we have different access levels for the network services. At the lower layers, we can access the simple sockets that allow us to use the connection-oriented and connectionless protocols like TCP or UDP, whereas other Python modules like *FTP* or *HTTP* are working on a higher layer – the *application layer*.

CREATING SOCKETS

In order to work with sockets in Python, we need to import the module *socket*.

```
import socket
```

Now, before we start defining and initializing our socket, we need to know a couple of things in advance:

- Are we using an internet socket or a UNIX socket?

- Which protocol are we going to use?

- Which IP-address are we using?

- Which port number are we using?

The first question can be answered quite simply. Since we want to communicate over a network instead of the operating system, we will stick with the *internet socket*.

The next question is a bit trickier. We choose between the protocols *TCP (*Transmission Control Protocol) and *UDP (*User Datagram Protocol). TCP is connection-oriented and more trustworthy than UDP. The chances of losing data are minimal in comparison to UDP. On the other hand, UDP is much faster than TCP. So the choice depends on the task we want to fulfil. For our examples, we will stick with

TCP since we don't care too much about speed for now.

The IP-address should be the address of the host our application will run on. For now, we will use *127.0.0.1* which is the *localhost* address. This applies to every machine. But notice that this only works when you are running your scripts locally.

For our port we can basically choose any number we want. But be careful with low numbers, since all numbers up to 1024 are *standardized* and all numbers from 1024 to 49151 are *reserved*. If you choose one of these numbers, you might have some conflicts with other applications or your operating system.

```
import socket

s = socket.socket(socket.AF_INET,
                  socket.SOCK_STREAM)
```

Here we created our first socket, by initializing an instance of the class *socket*. Notice that we passed two parameters here. The first one *AF_INET* states that we want an *internet socket* rather than a *UNIX socket*. The second one *SOCK_STREAM* is for the protocol that we choose. In this case it stands for *TCP*. If we wanted *UDP*, we would have to choose SOCK_DGRAM.

So we have a socket that uses the IP protocol (internet) and the TCP protocol. Now, before we get into the actual setup of the socket, we need to talk a little bit about clients and servers.

CLIENT-SERVER ARCHITECTURE

In a nutshell, the server is basically the one who provides information and *serves* data, whereas the clients are the ones who request and receive the data from the server.

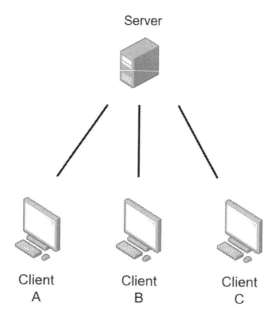

A server opens up a session with every client that connects to it. This way, servers are able to serve multiple clients at once and individually.

SERVER SOCKET METHODS

There are three methods of the *socket* class that are of high importance for the servers.

SERVER SOCKET METHODS	
METHOD	**DESCRIPTION**
bind()	Binds the address that consists of hostname and port to the socket
listen()	Waits for a message or a signal
accept()	Accepts the connection with a client

CLIENT SOCKET METHODS

For the client, there is only one specific and very important method, namely *connect*. With this method the client attempts to connect to a server which then has to *accept* this with the respective method.

OTHER SOCKET METHODS

Also, there are some other socket methods that are quite important in general.

OTHER SOCKET METHODS	
METHOD	**DESCRIPTION**
recv()	Receives a TCP message
send()	Sends a TCP message
recvfrom()	Receives a UDP message
sendto()	Sends a UDP message
close()	Closes a socket
gethostname()	Returns hostname of a socket

CREATING A SERVER

Now that we understand the client-server architecture, we are going to implement our server. We decided that we want to use TCP and an internet socket. For the address we will use the *localhost* address *127.0.0.1* and as a port, we will choose *9999*.

```
s = socket.socket(socket.AF_INET,
                  socket.SOCK_STREAM)
s.bind(("127.0.0.1", 9999))
s.listen()
print("Listening...")
```

Here we initialize our socket like we did in the beginning of this chapter. We then use the method *bind*, in order to assign the IP-address and the port we chose. Notice that we are passing a tuple as a parameter here. Last but not least, we put our socket to listening mode by using the method *listen*.

After that, we just have to create a loop that accepts the client requests that will eventually come in.

server.py

```python
import socket

s = socket.socket(socket.AF_INET,
                  socket.SOCK_STREAM)
s.bind(("127.0.0.1", 9999))
s.listen()
print("Listening...")

while True:
    client, address = s.accept()
    print("Connected to
{}".format(address))
    message = "Hello Client!"
    client.send(message.encode('ascii'))
    client.close()
```

The method *accept* waits for a connection attempt to come and accepts it. It then returns a *client* for responses and the *address* of the client that is connected. We can then use this client object in order to send the message. But it's important that we encode the message first, because otherwise we can't send it properly. At the end, we *close* the client because we don't need it anymore.

CREATING A CLIENT

Now our server is done and we just need some clients that connect to it. Our clients shall request a resource from the server. In this case, this is the message *"Hello Client!"*.

For our client we also need a socket but this time it will not use the function *bind* but the function *connect*. So let's start writing our code into a new file.

```python
import socket

s = socket.socket(socket.AF_INET,
                  socket.SOCK_STREAM)
s.connect(("127.0.0.1", 9999))
```

We just create an ordinary internet socket that uses TCP and then connect it to the localhost IP-address at the port 9999.

To now get the message from the server and decode it, we will use the *recv* function.

client.py

```python
import socket

s = socket.socket(socket.AF_INET,
                  socket.SOCK_STREAM)
s.connect(("127.0.0.1", 9999))
message = s.recv(1024)
s.close()
print(message.decode('ascii'))
```

After we connect to the server, we try to receive up to 1024 bytes from it. We then save the message into our variable and then we decode and print it.

CONNECTING SERVER AND CLIENT

Now in order to connect these two entities, we first need to run our server. If there is no server listening on the respective port, our client can't connect to anything. So we run our *server.py* script and start listening.

After that, we can run our *client.py* script many times and they will all connect to the server. The results will look like this:

Server

```
Listening...
Connected to ('127.0.0.1', 4935)
Connected to ('127.0.0.1', 4942)
Connected to ('127.0.0.1', 4943)
Connected to ('127.0.0.1', 4944)
Connected to ('127.0.0.1', 4945)
                    Client
Hello Client!
```

One thing you might optimize on that script if you want is the exception handling. If there is no server listening and our client tries to connect, we get a *ConnectionRefusedError* and our script crashes. Now you can fix this with the knowledge from the first book.

Hint: Use try and except!

PORT SCANNER

Now we have learned a lot about multithreading, locking, queues and sockets. With all that knowledge, we can create a highly efficient and well working *port scanner*.

What a port scanner basically does is: It tries to connect to certain ports at a host or a whole network, in order to find loopholes for future attacks. Open ports mean a security breach. And with our skills, we can already code our own penetration testing tool.

WARNING: *Port scanning is not allowed on any hosts or networks which you don't have explicit permission for. Only scan your own networks or networks for which you were given permission. I don't take any liability for what you do with this knowledge, since I warned you!*

```
import socket

target = "10.0.0.5"

def portscan(port):
```

```
try:
    s = socket.socket(socket.AF_INET,
                      socket.SOCK_STREAM)
    conn = s.connect((target, port))
    return True
except:
    return False

for x in range(1, 501):
    if(portscan(x)):
        print("Port {} is open!".format(x))
    else:
        print("Port {} is closed!".format(x))
```

So this scanner is quite simple. We define a target address. In this case, this is *10.0.0.5*. Our function *portscan* simply tries to connect to a certain port at that host. If it succeeds, the function returns *True*. If we get an error or an exception, it returns *False*.

This is as simple as a port scan can get. We then use a for loop to scan the first 500 ports and we always print if the port is open or closed.

Just choose a target address and run this script. You will see that it works.

```
Port 21 is closed!
Port 22 is open!
Port 23 is closed!
Port 24 is closed!
Port 25 is open!
```

But you will also notice that it is extremely slow. That's because we serially scan one port after the other. And I think we have already learned how to handle that.

THREADED PORT SCANNER

In order to speed up the scanning process, we are going to use *multithreading*. And to make sure that every port gets scanned and also that no port is scanned twice, we will use *queues*.

```python
import socket
from queue import Queue
import threading

target = "10.0.0.5"

q = Queue()
for x in range(1,501):
    q.put(x)

def portscan(port):
    try:
        s = socket.socket(socket.AF_INET,
                          socket.SOCK_STREAM)
        conn = s.connect((target, port))
        return True
    except:
        return False

def worker():
    while True:
        port = q.get()
        if portscan(port):
            print("Port {} is open!"
                  .format(port))
```

So we start by creating a queue and filling it up with all numbers from 1 to 500. We then have two functions. The *portscan* function does the scanning itself and the *worker* function gets all the ports from the queue in order to pass them to the *portscan* function and prints the result. In order to not get confused with the output, we only print when a port is open because we don't care when a port is closed.

Now we just have to decide how many threads we want to start and then we can go for it.

```
for x in range(30):
    t = threading.Thread(target=worker)
    t.start()
```

In this example, we start 30 threads at the same time. If you run this, you will see that it increases the scanning speed a lot. Within a few seconds, all the 500 ports are scanned. So if you want, you can increase the number to 5000.

The results for my virtual server are the following:

```
Port 25 is open!
Port 22 is open!
Port 80 is open!
Port 110 is open!
Port 119 is open!
Port 143 is open!
Port 443 is open!
Port 465 is open!
```

As you can see, there are a lot of vulnerabilities here. You now just have to google which ports are interesting and depending on your side you may either prepare for an attack or fix the security breaches. For example port 22 is SSH and quite dangerous.

5 – Database Programming

Databases are one of the most popular ways to store and manage data in computer science. Because of that, in this chapter we are going to take a look at database programming with Python.

Notice that for most databases we use the query language *SQL*, which stands for *Structured Query Language*. We use this language in order to manage the database, the tables and the rows and columns. This chapter is not about database structure itself, nor is it about SQL. Maybe I will write a specific SQL book in the future but here we are only going to focus on the implementation in Python. We are not going to explain the SQL syntax in too much detail.

Connecting to SQLite

The database that comes pre-installed with Python is called *SQLite*. It is also the one which we are going to use. Of course, there are also other libraries for *MySQL, MongoDB* etc.

In order to use *SQLite* in Python, we need to import the respective module – *sqlite3*.

```
import sqlite3
```

Now, to create a new database file on our disk, we need to use the *connect* method.

```
conn = sqlite3.connect('mydata.db')
```

This right here creates the new file *mydata.db* and connects to this database. It returns a connection object which we save in the variable *conn*.

EXECUTING STATEMENTS

So, we have established a connection to the database. But in order to execute *SQL* statements, we will need to create a so-called *cursor*.

```
c = conn.cursor()
```

We get this cursor by using the method *cursor* of our connection object that returns it. Now we can go ahead and execute all kinds of statements.

CREATING TABLES

For example, we can create our first table like this:

```
c.execute("""CREATE TABLE persons (
            first_name TEXT,
            last_name TEXT,
            age INTEGER
            )""")
```

Here we use the *execute* function and write our query. What we are passing here is SQL code. As I already said, understanding SQL is not the main objective here. We are focusing on the Python part. Nevertheless, it's quite obvious what's happening here. We are creating a new *table* with the name *persons* and each person will have the three attributes *first_name, last_name* and *age*.

Now our statement is written but in order to really execute it, we ne need to commit to our connection.

```
conn.commit()
```

When we do this, our statement gets executed and our table created. Notice that this works only once, since after that the table already exists and can't be created again.

At the end, don't forget to close the connection, when you are done with everything.

```
conn.close()
```

INSERTING VALUES

Now let's fill up our table with some values. For this, we just use an ordinary *INSERT* statement.

```
c.execute("""INSERT INTO persons VALUES
             ('John', 'Smith', 25),
             ('Anna', 'Smith', 30),
             ('Mike', 'Johnson', 40)""")

conn.commit()
conn.close()
```

So basically, we are just adding three entries to our table. When you run this code, you will see that everything went fine. But to be on the safe side, we will try to now extract the values from the database into our program.

In order to get values from the database, we need to first execute a *SELECT* statement. After that, we also need to *fetch* the results.

```
c.execute("""SELECT * FROM persons
             WHERE last_name = 'Smith'""")

print(c.fetchall())

conn.commit()
conn.close()
```

As you can see, our *SELECT* statement that gets all the entries where the *last_name* has the value *Smith*. We then need to use the method *fetchall* of the cursor, in order to get our results. It returns a list of tuples, where every tuple is one entry. Alternatively, we could use the method *fetchone* to only get the first entry or *fetchmany* to get a specific amount of entries. In our case however, the result looks like this:

```
[('John', 'Smith', 25), ('Anna', 'Smith', 30)]
```

CLASSES AND TABLES

Now in order to make the communication more efficient and easier, we are going to create a *Person* class that has the columns as attributes.

```python
class Person():

    def __init__(self, first=None,
                 last=None, age=None):
        self.first = first
        self.last = last
        self.age = age

    def clone_person(self, result):
        self.first = result[0]
        self.last = result[1]
        self.age = result[2]
```

Here we have a constructor with default parameters. In case we don't specify any values, they get assigned the value *None*. Also, we have a function *clone_person* that gets passed a sequence and assigns the values of it to the object. In our case, this sequence will be the tuple from the *fetching* results.

FROM TABLE TO OBJECT

So let's create a new *Person* object by getting its data from our database.

```python
c.execute("""SELECT * FROM persons
            WHERE last_name = 'Smith'""")

person1 = Person()
person1.clone_person(c.fetchone())

print(person1.first)
print(person1.last)
print(person1.age)
```

Here we fetch the first entry of our query results, by using the *fetchone* function. The result is the following:

```
John
Smith
25
```

FROM OBJECT TO TABLE

We can also do that the other way around. Let's create a person objects, assign values to the attributes and then insert this object into our database.

```python
person2 = Person("Bob", "Davis", 23)

c.execute("""INSERT INTO persons VALUES
        ('{}', '{}', '{}')"""
        .format(person2.first,
                person2.last,
                person2.age))

conn.commit()
conn.close()
```

Here we used the basic *format* function in order to put our values into the statement. When we execute it, our object gets inserted into the database. We can check this by printing all objects of the table *persons*.

```python
c.execute("SELECT * FROM persons")
print(c.fetchall())
```

In the results, we find our new object:

```
[('John', 'Smith', 25), ('Anna', 'Smith', 30),
('Mike', 'Johnson', 40), ('Bob', 'Davis', 23)]
```

PREPARED STATEMENTS

There is a much more secure and elegant way to put the values of our attributes into the SQL statements. We can use *prepared statements*.

```
person = Person("Julia", "Johnson", 28)

c.execute("INSERT INTO persons VALUES (?, ?,
?)",
          (person.first, person.last,
person.age))

conn.commit()
conn.close()
```

We replace the values with question marks and pass the values as a tuple in the function. This makes our statements cleaner and also less prone to SQL injections.

MORE ABOUT SQL

For this book, we are done with database programming. But there's a lot more to learn about SQL and databases. As I said, I might publish a detailed SQL book in the future so keep checking my author page on Amazon.

However, if you are interested in learning SQL right now, you can check out the W3Schools tutorial.

W3Schools: https://www.w3schools.com/sql/

6 – RECURSION

In this short chapter, we are going to talk about a programming concept that I would say should be taught in a book for intermediates. This concept is *recursion* and basically it refers to a function calling itself.

```
def function():
    function()

function()
```

So what do you think happens, when you call a function like that? It is a function that calls itself. And this called function calls itself again and so on. Basically, you get into an endless recursion. This is not very useful and in Python we get an *RecursionError* when the maximum recursion depth is exceeded.

Every program has a stack memory and this memory is limited. When we run a function we allocate stack memory space and if there is no space left, this is called *Stack Overflow*. This is also where the name of the famous forum comes from.

FACTORIAL CALCULATION

But recursion can also be useful, if it's managed right. For example, we can write a recursive function that calculates the *factorial* of a number. A factorial is just the value you get, when you multiply a number by every lower whole number down to one.

So 10 factorial would be 10 times 9 times 8 and so on until you get to times 1.

```
def factorial(n):
    if n < 1:
        return 1
    else:
        number = n * factorial(n-1)
        return number
```

Look at this function. When we first call it, the parameter *n* is our base number that we want to calculate the factorial of. If *n* is not smaller than one, we multiply it by the factorial of *n-1*. At the end, we return the number.

Notice that our first function call doesn't return anything until we get down to one. This is because it always calls itself in itself over and over again. At the end all the results are multiplied by the last *return* which of course is *one*. Finally, we can print the end result.

This might be quite confusing, if you have never heard of recursion before. Just take your time and analyze what's happening step-by-step here. Try to play around with this concept of *recursion*.

7 – XML Processing

Up until now, we either saved our data into regular text files or into professional databases. Sometimes however, our script is quite small and doesn't need a big database but we still want to structure our data in files. For this, we can use *XML*.

XML stands for *Extensible Markup Language* and is a language that allows us to hierarchically structure our data in files. It is platform-independent and also application-independent. XML files that you create with a Python script, can be read and processed by a C++ or Java application.

XML Parser

In Python, we can choose between two modules for *parsing* XML files – *SAX* and *DOM*.

Simple API for XML (SAX)

SAX stands for *Simple API for XML* and is better suited for large XML files or in situations where we have very limited RAM memory space. This is because in this mode we never load the full file into our RAM. We read the file from our hard drive and only load the little parts that we need right at the moment into the RAM. An additional effect of this is that we can only read from the file and not manipulate it and change values.

Document Object Model (DOM)

DOM stands for *Document Object Model* and is the generally recommended option. It is a language-independent API for working with XML. Here we always load the full XML file into our RAM and then save it there in a hierarchical structure. Because of that, we can use all of the features and also manipulate the file.

Obviously, DOM is a lot faster than SAX because it is using the RAM instead of the hard disk. The main memory is way more efficient than the hard drive. We only use SAX when our RAM is so limited that we can't even load the full XML file into it without problems.

There is no reason to not use both options in the same projects. We can choose depending on the use case.

XML Structure

For this chapter, we are going to use the following XML file:

```xml
<?xml version="1.0"?>
<group>
    <person id="1">
        <name>John Smith</name>
        <age>20</age>
        <weight>80</weight>
        <height>188</height>
    </person>
    <person id="2">
        <name>Mike Davis</name>
        <age>45</age>
        <weight>82</weight>
        <height>185</height>
    </person>
    <person id="3">
        <name>Anna Johnson</name>
        <age>33</age>
        <weight>67</weight>
        <height>167</height>
    </person>
    <person id="4">
        <name>Bob Smith</name>
        <age>60</age>
        <weight>70</weight>
        <height>174</height>
    </person>
    <person id="5">
        <name>Sarah Pitt</name>
        <age>12</age>
        <weight>50</weight>
        <height>152</height>
    </person>
</group>
```

As you can see, the structure is quite simple. The first row is just a notation and indicates that we are using XML version one. After that we have various tags. Every tag that gets opened also gets closed at the end.

Basically, we have one *group* tag. Within that, we have multiple *person* tags that all have the attribute *id*. And then again, every *person* has four tags with their values. These tags are the attributes of the respective person. We save this file as *group.xml*.

XML WITH SAX

In order to work with *SAX,* we first need to import the module:

```
import xml.sax
```

Now, what we need in order to process the XML data is a *content handler*. It handles and processes the attributes and tags of the file.

```
import xml.sax

handler = xml.sax.ContentHandler()

parser = xml.sax.make_parser()
parser.setContentHandler(handler)
parser.parse("group.xml")
```

First we create an instance of the *ContentHandler* class. Then we use the method *make_parser,* in order to create a *parser* object. After that, we set our *handler* to the content handler of our parser. We can then parse the file by using the method *parse*.

Now, when we execute our script, we don't see anything. This is because we need to define what happens when an element gets parsed.

Content Handler Class

For this, we will define our own *content handler* class.
Let's start with a very simple example.

```python
import xml.sax

class GroupHandler(xml.sax.ContentHandler):
    def startElement(self, name, attrs):
        print(name)

handler = GroupHandler()
parser = xml.sax.make_parser()
parser.setContentHandler(handler)
parser.parse("group.xml")
```

We created a class *GroupHandler* that inherits from
ContentHandler. Then we overwrite the function
startElement. Every time an element gets processed,
this function gets called. So by manipulating it, we
can define what shall happen during the parsing
process.

Notice that the function has two parameters – *name*
and *attr*. These represent the tag name and the
attributes. In our simple example, we just print the tag
names. So, let's get to a more interesting example.

Processing XML Data

The following example is a bit more complex and
includes two more functions.

```python
import xml.sax

class GroupHandler(xml.sax.ContentHandler):
```

```python
    def startElement(self, name, attrs):
        self.current = name
        if self.current == "person":
            print("--- Person ---")
            id = attrs["id"]
            print("ID: %s" % id)

    def endElement(self, name):
        if self.current == "name":
            print("Name: %s" % self.name)
        elif self.current == "age":
            print("Age: %s" % self.age)
        elif self.current == "weight":
            print("Weight: %s" % self.weight)
        elif self.current == "height":
            print("Height: %s" % self.height)
        self.current = ""

    def characters(self, content):
        if self.current == "name":
            self.name = content
        elif self.current == "age":
            self.age = content
        elif self.current == "weight":
            self.weight = content
        elif self.current == "height":
            self.height = content

handler = GroupHandler()
parser = xml.sax.make_parser()
parser.setContentHandler(handler)
parser.parse("group.xml")
```

The first thing you will notice here is that we have three functions instead of one. When we start processing an element, the function *startElement* gets called. Then we go on to process the individual *characters* which are *name, age, weight* and *height*. At the end of the element parsing, we call the *endElement* function.

In this example, we first check if the element is a *person* or not. If this is the case we print the *id* just for information. We then go on with the *characters* method. It checks which tag belongs to which attribute and saves the values accordingly. At the end, we print out all the values. This is what the results look like:

```
--- Person ---
ID: 1
Name: John Smith
Age: 20
Weight: 80
Height: 188
--- Person ---
ID: 2
Name: Mike Davis
Age: 45
Weight: 82
Height: 185
--- Person ---
...
```

XML WITH DOM

Now, let's look at the DOM option. Here we can not only read from XML files but also change values and attributes. In order to work with DOM, we again need to import the respective module.

```
import xml.dom.minidom
```

When working with DOM, we need to create a so-called *DOM-Tree* and view all elements as collections or sequences.

```
domtree = xml.dom.minidom.parse("group.xml")
group = domtree.documentElement
```

We parse the XML file by using the method *parse*. This returns a DOM-tree, which we save into a variable. Then we get the *documentElement* of our tree and in our case this is *group*. We also save this one into an object.

```
persons = group.getElementsByTagName("person")

for person in persons:
    print("--- Person ---")
    if person.hasAttribute("id"):
        print("ID: %s" %
person.getAttribute("id"))

    name =
person.getElementsByTagName("name")[0]
    age = person.getElementsByTagName("age")[0]
    weight =
person.getElementsByTagName("weight")[0]
    height =
person.getElementsByTagName("height")[0]
```

Now, we can get all the individual elements by using the *getElementsByTagName* function. For example, we save all our *person* tags into a variable by using this method and specifying the name of our desired tags. Our *persons* variable is now a sequence that we can iterate over.

By using the functions *hasAttribute* and *getAttribute,* we can also access the attributes of our tags. In this case, this is only the *id*. In order to get the tag values of the individual person, we again use the method *getElementsByTagName*.

When we do all that and execute our script, we get the exact same result as with *SAX*.

```
--- Person ---
ID: 1
Name: John Smith
Age: 20
Weight: 80
Height: 188
--- Person ---
ID: 2
Name: Mike Davis
Age: 45
Weight: 82
Height: 185
--- Person ---
...
```

MANIPULATING XML FILES

Since we are now working with *DOM*, let's manipulate our XML file and change some values.

```
persons = group.getElementsByTagName("person")

persons[0].getElementsByTagName("name")[0].childNod
es[0].nodeValue = "New Name"
```

As you can see, we are using the same function, to access our elements. Here we adress the *name* tag of the first *person* object. Then we need to access the *childNodes* and change their *nodeValue*. Notice that we only have one element *name* and also only one child node but we still need to address the index zero, for the first element.

In this example, we change the name of the first person to *New Name*. Now in order to apply these changes to the real file, we need to write into it.

```
domtree.writexml(open("group.xml", "w"))
```

We use the *writexml* method of our initial *domtree* object. As a parameter, we pass a file stream that writes into our XML file. After doing that, we can look at the changes.

```
<person id="1">
    <name>New Name</name>
    <age>20</age>
    <weight>80</weight>
    <height>188</height>
</person>
```

We can also change the attributes by using the function *setAttribute*.

```
persons[0].setAttribute("id", "10")
```

Here we change the attribute *id* of the first person to *10*.

```
<person id="10">
    <name>New Name</name>
    <age>20</age>
    <weight>80</weight>
    <height>188</height>
</person>
```

CREATING NEW ELEMENTS

The last thing that we are going to look at in this chapter is creating new XML elements by using DOM. In order to do that, we first need to define a new *person* element.

```
newperson = domtree.createElement("person")
newperson.setAttribute("id", "6")
```

So we use the *domtree* object and the respective method, to create a new XML element. Then we set the *id* attribute to the next number.

After that, we create all the elements that we need for the person and assign values to them.

```
name = domtree.createElement("name")
name.appendChild(domtree.createTextNode("Paul
Smith"))

age = domtree.createElement("age")
age.appendChild(domtree.createTextNode("45"))

weight = domtree.createElement("weight")
weight.appendChild(domtree.createTextNode("78"))

height = domtree.createElement("height")
height.appendChild(domtree.createTextNode("178"))
```

First, we create a new element for each attribute of the person. Then we use the method *appendChild* to put something in between the tags of our element. In this case we create a new *TextNode*, which is basically just text.

Last but not least, we again need to use the method *appendChild* in order to define the hierarchical structure. The attribute elements are the childs of the *person* element and this itself is the child of the *group* element.

```
newperson.appendChild(name)
newperson.appendChild(age)
newperson.appendChild(weight)
newperson.appendChild(height)

group.appendChild(newperson)

domtree.writexml(open("group.xml", "w"))
```

When we write these changes into our file, we can see the following results:

```
<person id="6">
    <name>Paul Smith</name>
    <age>45</age>
    <weight>78</weight>
    <height>178</height>
</person>
```

8 – LOGGING

No matter what we do in computer science, sooner or later we will need logs. Every system that has a certain size produces errors or conditions in which specific people should be warned or informed. Nowadays, everything gets logged or recorded. Bank transactions, flights, networking activities, operating systems and much more. Log files help us to find problems and to get information about the state of our systems. They are an essential tool for avoiding and understanding errors.

Up until now, we have always printed some message onto the console screen when we encountered an error. But when our applications grow, this becomes confusing and we need to categorize and outsource our logs. In addition, not every message is equally relevant. Some messages are urgent because a critical component fails and some just provide nice information.

SECURITY LEVELS

In Python, we have got five security levels. A higher level means higher importance or urgency.

1. DEBUG
2. INFO
3. WARNING
4. ERROR
5. CRITICAL

Notice that when we choose a certain security level, we also get all the messages of the levels above. So for example, *INFO* also prints the messages of *WARNING, ERROR* and *CRITICAL* but not of *DEBUG*.

DEBUG is mainly used for tests, experiments or in order to check something. We typically use this mode, when we are looking for errors (troubleshooting).

We use *INFO* when we want to log all the important events that inform us about what is happening. This might be something like *"User A logged in successfully!"* or *"Now we have 17 users online!"*

WARNING messages are messages that inform us about irregularities and things that might go wrong and become a problem. For example messages like *"Only 247 MB of RAM left!"*

An *ERROR* message gets logged or printed when something didn't go according to the plan. When we get an exception this is a classical error.

CRITICAL messages tell us that critical for the whole system or application happened. This might be the case when a crucial component fails and we have to immediately stop all operations.

CREATING LOGGERS

In order to create a logger in Python, we need to import the *logging* module.

```
import logging
```

Now we can just log messages by directly using the respective functions of the *logging* module.

```
logging.info("First informational
message!")
logging.critical("This is serious!")
```

This works because we are using the *root* logger. We haven't created our own loggers yet. The output looks like this:

```
CRITICAL:root:This is serious!
INFO:root:Logger successfully created!
```

So let's create our own logger now. This is done by either using the constructor of the *Logger* class or by using the method *getLogger*.

```
logger = logging.getLogger()
logger = logging.Logger("MYLOGGER")
```

Notice that we need to specify a name for our logger, if we use the constructor. Now we can log our messages.

```
logger.info("Logger successfully created!")
logger.log(logging.INFO, "Successful!")
logger.critical("Critical Message!")
logger.log(logging.CRITICAL, "Critical!")
```

Here we also have two different options for logging messages. We can either directly call the function of the respective security level or we can use the method *log* and specify the security level in the parameters.

But when you now execute the script, you will notice that it will only print the critical messages. This has two reasons. First of all, we need to adjust the level of the logger and second of all, we need to remove all of the *handlers* from the default *root* logger.

```
for handler in logging.root.handlers:
    logging.root.removeHandler(handler)
logging.basicConfig(level=logging.INFO)
```

Here we just use a for loop in order to remove all the handlers from the root logger. Then we use the *basicConfig* method, in order to set our logging level to *INFO*. When we now run our code again, the output is the following:

```
INFO:MYLOGGER:Logger successfully created!
INFO:MYLOGGER:Successful!
CRITICAL:MYLOGGER:Critical Message!
CRITICAL:MYLOGGER:Critical!
```

LOGGING INTO FILES

What we are mainly interested in is logging into files. For this, we need a so-called *FileHandler*. It is an object that we add to our logger, in order to make it log everything into a specific file.

```python
import logging

logger = logging.getLogger("MYLOGGER")
logger.setLevel(logging.INFO)

handler =
logging.FileHandler("logfile.log")
handler.setLevel(logging.INFO)

logger.addHandler(handler)
logger.info("Log this into the file!")
logger.critical("This is critical!")
```

We start again by defining a logger. Then we set the security level to *INFO* by using the function *setLevel*. After that, we create a *FileHandler* that logs into the file *logfile.log*. Here we also need to set the security level. Finally, we add the handler to our logger using the *addHandler* function and start logging messages.

FORMATTING LOGS

One thing that you will notice is that we don't have any format in our logs. We don't know which logger was used or which security level our message has. For this, we can use a so-called *formatter*.

```python
import logging

logger = logging.getLogger()
logger.setLevel(logging.INFO)

handler =
logging.FileHandler("logfile.log")
handler.setLevel(logging.INFO)

formatter = logging.Formatter('%(asctime)s:
%(levelname)s - %(message)s')
handler.setFormatter(formatter)

logger.addHandler(handler)
logger.info("This will get into the file!")
```

We create a formatter by using the constructor of the respective class. Then we use the keywords for the timestamp, the security level name and the message. Last but not least, we assign the formatter to our handler and start logging again. When we now look into our file, we will find a more detailed message.

```
2019-06-25 15:41:43,523: INFO - This will get into the
file!
```

These log messages can be very helpful, if they are used wisely. Place them wherever something important or alarming happens in your code.

9 – REGULAR EXPRESSIONS

In programming, you will oftentimes have to deal with long texts from which we want to extract specific information. Also, when we want to process certain inputs, we need to check for a specific pattern. For example, think about emails. They need to have some text, followed by an @ character, then again some text and finally a *dot* and again some little text.

In order to make the validations easier, more efficient and more compact, we use so-called *regular expressions*.

The topic of regular expressions is very huge and you could write a whole book only about it. This is why we are not going to focus too much on the various placeholders and patterns of the expressions themselves but on the implementation of *RegEx* in Python.

So in order to confuse you right in the beginning, let's look at a regular expression that checks if the format of an email-address is valid.

```
^[a-zA-Z0-9.!#$%&'*+/=?^_`{|}~-]+@[a-zA-Z0-
9](?:[a-zA-Z0-9-]{0,61}[a-zA-Z0-9])?(?:\.[a-zA-
Z0-9](?:[a-zA-Z0-9-]{0,61}[a-zA-Z0-9])?)*$
```

Now you can see why this is a huge field to learn. In this chapter, we are not going to build regular expressions like this. We are going to focus on quite simple examples and how to properly implement them in Python.

IDENTIFIER

Let's get started with some basic knowledge first. So-called *identifiers* define what kind of character should be at a certain place. Here you have some examples:

|REGEX IDENTIFIERS	
IDENTIFIER	**DESCRIPTION**
\d	Some digit
\D	Everything BUT a digit
\s	White space
\S	Everything BUT a white space
\w	Some letter
\W	Everything BUT a letter
.	Every character except for new lines
\b	White spaces around a word
\.	A dot

MODIFIER

The *modifiers* extend the regular expressions and the identifiers. They might be seen as some kind of operator for regular expressions.

REGEX MODIFIERS	
MODIFIER	**DESCRIPTION**
{x,y}	A number that has a length between x and y
+	At least one
?	None or one
*	Everything
$	At the end of a string
^	At the beginning of a string
|	Either Or Example: x | y = either x or y
[]	Value range
{x}	x times
{x,y}	x to y times

Escape Characters

Last but not least, we have the classic *escape characters*.

REGEX ESCAPE CHARATCERS	
CHARACTER	**DESCRIPTION**
\n	New Line
\t	Tab
\s	White Space

APPLYING REGULAR EXPRESSIONS

FINDING STRINGS

In order to apply these regular expressions in Python, we need to import the module *re*.

```
import re
```

Now we can start by trying to find some patterns in our strings.

```
text = '''
Mike is 20 years old and George is 29!
My grandma is even 104 years old!
'''

ages = re.findall(r'\d{1,3}', text)
print(ages)
```

In this example, we have a text with three ages in it. What we want to do is to filter these out and print them separately.

As you can see, we use the function *findall* in order to apply the regular expression onto our string. In this case, we are looking for numbers that are one to three digits long. Notice that we are using an *r* character before we write our expression. This indicates that the given string is a regular expression.

At the end, we print our result and get the following output:

```
['20', '29', '104']
```

MATCHING STRINGS

What we can also do is to check if a string matches a certain regular expression. For example, we can apply our regular expression for mails here.

```python
import re

text = "test@mail.com"

result = re.fullmatch(r"^[a-zA-Z0-
9.!#$%&'*+/=?^_`{|}~-]+@[a-zA-Z0-9](?:[a-
zA-Z0-9-]{0,61}[a-zA-Z0-9])?(?:\.[a-zA-Z0-
9](?:[a-zA-Z0-9-]{0,61}[a-zA-Z0-9])?)*$",
text)

if result != None:
    print("VALID!")
else:
    print("INVALID!")
```

We are not going to talk about the regular expression itself here. It is very long and complicated. But what we see here is a new function called *fullmatch*. This function returns the checked string if it matches the regular expression. In this case, this happens when the string has a valid mail format.

If the expression doesn't match the string, the function returns *None*. In our example above, we get the message *"VALID!"* since the expression is met. If we enter something like *"Hello World!",* we will get the other message.

MANIPULATING STRINGS

Finally, we are going to take a look at manipulating strings with regular expressions. By using the function *sub* we can replace all the parts of a string that match the expression by something else.

```python
import re

text = """
Mike is 20 years old and George is 29!
My grandma is even 104 years old!
"""

text = re.sub(r'\d{1,3}', "100", text)
print(text)
```

In this example, we replace all ages by *100*. This is what gets printed:

```
Mike is 100 years old and George is 100!
My grandma is even 100 years old!
```

These are the basic functions that we can operate with in Python when dealing with regular expressions. If you want to learn more about regular expressions just google and you will find a lot of guides. Play around with the identifiers and modifiers a little bit until you feel like you understand how they work.

WHAT'S NEXT?

Now you have finished reading the second volume of this Python Bible series. This one was way more complex than the first one and it had a lot more content. Make sure that you practice what you've learned. If necessary, reread this book a couple of times and play around with the code samples. That will dramatically increase the value that you can get out of this book.

However, you are now definitely able to develop some advanced and professional Python applications. You can develop a chat, a port scanner, a string formatter and many more ideas. But this is still just the beginning. Even though you can now consider yourself to be an advanced Python programmer, there is much more to learn.

With the next volumes we are going to dive deep into the fields of machine learning, data science and finance. By having read the first two volumes you already have an excellent basis and I encourage you to continue your journey. I hope you could get some value out of this book and that it helped you to become a better programmer. So stay tuned and read the next volume about Data Science!

Last but not least, a little reminder. This book was written for you, so that you can get as much value as possible and learn to code effectively. If you find this book valuable or you think you learned something new, please write a quick review on Amazon. It is completely free and takes about one minute. But it helps me produce more high quality books, which you can benefit from.

Thank you!

NeuralNine

If you are interested in free educational content about programming and machine learning, check out https://www.neuralnine.com/

There we have free blog posts, videos and more for you! Also, you can follow the ***@neuralnine*** Instagram account for daily infographics about programming and AI!

Website: https://www.neuralnine.com/

Instagram: @neuralnine

YouTube: NeuralNine

Made in the USA
Middletown, DE
08 August 2023